Los Angeles

Los Angeles

Concept and Design: Robert D. Shangle
Text: Brian Berger

First Printing September, 1980
Published by Beautiful America Publishing Company
P.O. Box 608, Beaverton, Oregon 97075
Robert D. Shangle, Publisher

Library of Congress Cataloging in Publication Data
Los Angeles—Commemorating 200 Years
1. Los Angeles—Description—Views. I. Title.
F869.L843B47   917.94 94   80-16824
ISBN 0-89802-176-6

Photo Credits

ROY BISHOP—*page 18, pages 20-21, page 24, page 27, page 28, page 32, page 34, page 39, page 44, page 47, page 50, pages 52-53, page 54, page 58, page 59, page 61, page 64, page 69, page 70, page 71, page 76, page 77, page 78, page 80, pages 84-85, page 86, page 88, page 95, page 97, page 99, page 101, page 108, page 111, page 112, page 114, page 115, pages 116-117, page 123, page 125, page 127, page 134, page 139, page 142.*

JAMES BLANK—*page 19, page 22, page 30, page 31, page 35, page 36, page 38, page 42, page 43, page 45, page 46, page 48, page 49, page 55, page 57, page 60, page 62, page 63, page 65, page 66, page 68, pages 72-73, page 74, page 79, page 82, page 83, page 87, page 89, page 91, page 92, page 93, page 96, page 98, page 103, page 106, page 107, page 109, page 110, page 113, page 118, page 119, page 121, page 124, page 128, page 131.*

JOHN HILL—*page 94, page 100, pages 104-105, page 130.*

ROY MURPHY—*page 33, pages 40-41, page 67.*

ROBERT SHANGLE—*page 17, page 23, page 25, page 26, page 29, page 37, page 51, page 56, page 75, page 81, page 90, page 102, page 120, page 122, page 126, page 135, page 138, page 143.*

Manufactured by
Hiller Industries
631 North 400 West
Salt Lake City, Utah USA

Color Separations
by
Universal Color Corporation
Beaverton, Oregon / San Diego, California

Enlarged Prints

Most of the photography in this book is available as photographic enlargements.
Send self-addressed, stamped envelope for information.
For a complete catalog, send $1.00.
Beautiful America Publishing Company
P.O. Box 608
Beaverton, Oregon 97075

Contents

Introduction

It's been said, the only thing that remains constant in Los Angeles is its *constant* state of flux. For most Angelenos, the city's ever-changing face has become an accepted, and looked-forward-to, phenomena. There is an atmosphere of immediacy about this sprawling megalopolis that causes its residents to believe that whatever is happening of importance in the world, it is happening within Los Angeles' 463-square-mile area. Daily, Angelenos watch and listen to the city grow, even as they see parts of her die—the old sacrificed for the new—knowing that what is a great city today, will become a greater city tomorrow.

For years Los Angeles' growth was like the spreading of a thick pancake batter, slowly oozing outward, in an ever-widening circle. But, today, that growth is upward. Los Angeles has an awesome pattern of flux. No longer a city in want of an identifiable ''center,'' her core area now sprouts 50- and 60-story monoliths of steel and tinted glass. Fountains spring from the centers of neatly landscaped malls. A subterranean shopping center (the world's largest) draws thousands daily to browse through the more than 50 shops that occupy its two levels.

Like the constant division of cells required to form a growing fetus, the city's population has swelled to three million—double its mid-'40s figure. Where farmlands once covered great sections of suburban areas, there has been a doubling or tripling of population figures every decade, adding another seven million persons to the Los Angeles County area. Seen from the air, Los Angeles appears as a vast outpouring of humanity, barely contained by a group of basin-forming mountains.

The only direction Los Angeles has not spread is west, halted by the waters of the Pacific Ocean. From Malibu, near the western end of the Santa Monica Mountains, to Laguna Beach, far to the southeast of the city, no one section along Greater Los Angeles' miles of waterfront can be called its Gold Coast; it's *all* gold. Such is the demand for this choice real estate that one could buy a small spread in Texas for the price necessary to own a two-bedroom condominium anywhere overlooking the water. The tempo along the boardwalks is of the 24-hour, non-stop variety: roller skaters, joggers, pantomimists and party-goers, just to name a few, who add to the excitement of the area.

Northwest of the Civic Center, another area of nonstop activity flashes its mesmerizing lure—Hollywood. Here the Saturday matinee was created. One could be frightened twice: once in the theatre, and later when your mother turned off your bedroom light. Hollywood was the ornate, motion picture palace of Grauman's (now Mann's) Chinese Theatre with its star-inscribed sidewalks. It was cruising Hollywood Boulevard or the ''Strip'' on a Saturday night. It was world premiers and a chance to catch a glimpse of a movie star. Hollywood was a place to see and be seen. It was all this, and still is.

It is hard for a visitor to get a grip on this city. Even native Angelenos will agree that size precludes any narrow definitions of its nature. Los Angeles is mountains, desert, and sea. It is oil production and aerospace technology; futuristic buildings and eateries shaped like giant hotdogs or hamburgers; 1,500 miles of freeways and 3.5 million cars. It is West Hollywood, Beverly Hills, and $100,000 Rolls-Royce convertibles parked in front of the posh clothiers and jewelry stores along Rodeo Drive. It is the San Fernando Valley, with its thousands of turquoise-tinted swimming pools and a third of Los Angeles' population; Pasadena's Colorado Boulevard on New Year's Day, with a million flowers covering miles of parade floats.

Los Angeles is Simon Rodia's ''Watts Towers'' with their steel, shell and glass spires, an immigrant's gift to the United States because ''. . . there are nice people in this country.'' It is Arcadia's beautifully landscaped Santa Anita Racetrack, backdropped by the rugged San Gabriel Mountains; children wearing Mickey Mouse ears and carrying balloons that say Disneyland; Santa Monica's Gold's Gym, a mecca for body building. Los Angeles is 350 days of sunshine and hot Santa Anita winds; it is air-conditioned dog and cat hotels, and animal psychologists. It is living-hair transplants and creative cosmetic surgery. Los Angeles is closets full of jogging shoes, hiking boots, tennis rackets, and Frisbees; audience participation in daytime television game shows; young millionaire movie producers, and thousands of aspiring actors, selling shoes or waiting on tables.

As far back as 1944, Paul Schrecker, writing for *Harper's*, expressed what could very well be a current appraisal of Los Angeles when he wrote: ''The city seems not like a real city resulting from natural growth, but like an agglomeration of many variegated movie sets, which stand alongside one another but have no connection with one another. Hardly anything looks as if it had struck roots under the surface.''

It is this changing quality that has made the Los Angeles image difficult to capture—whether with words, or pictures. Yet with the text and pictures in this book, we have stopped the clock on 200 years of Los Angeles' growth, and in anticipation of its varying nature, taken a peek at its possible future.

Brian Berger

Mission To Megalopolis

September 28, 1542, two small galleons dropped anchor in the harbor at San Diego. Their crews, commanded by the Portuguese captain Juan Rodriquez Cabrillo, were sailing under the flag of Spain in search of a sea passage through the North American continent. The mythical Strait of Anian (the Northwest Passage) would elude them, but their voyage marked the first efforts of white men to explore the coast of Upper California.

Cabrillo found little about this new land to excite his imagination. Other than the fine harbor at San Diego, which he named San Miguel, the land appeared much the same as the dry interior of Baja (lower) California. There were no cities of gold, little water, and curious Indians. To worsen matters, Cabrillo sustained a bad break of his upper arm. For three months following the accident, he was troubled by continuous pain, the result of an infection, which finally claimed his life. It was left to his chief pilot, Bartolome Ferrelo, to lead the two ships back to their home port of Navidad. Upon their return, the half-starved and scurvy-ridden crews reported to Viceroy Mendoza the dismal results of their mission. It ended Spain's immediate interests in the new territory.

More than 200 years passed before Captain Gaspar de Portola, leading a tired company of dust-ridden soldiers overland from Mexico, established Spanish rule in Upper California. Portola's journey had taken him through San Diego and then northward along the coast into the area that is now Orange County. Here, along the west bank of the Los Angeles River, the party entered the Indian village of Yang-na. Upon establishing friendly relations with these native Californians, Portola and his men departed. Two years later, the Spanish returned, founding Mission San Gabriel on a spot just east of the village.

Hoping to attract settlers to the area, Felipe de Neve (the first Governor of California) circulated the word through northern Mexico that he was offering ''free land, horse, and farm animals, a plow and other tools, and ten dollars per month in wages'' for men of the soil. His generosity drew 11 men to a newly chosen pueblo site a short distance west of Mission San Gabriel. On September 4, 1781, the men and their families gathered around the site to witness a blessing of the lots by a San Gabriel padre. The name given was *El Pueblo de Nuestra Senora La Reina de Los Angeles*— The Town of Our Lady, the Queen of the Angels.

From the first rude beginnings marking this site of the future city of Los Angeles, the Spaniards expanded their foothold in California. Over the next 42 years, 21 missions, at least four military garrisons, 30 ranchos (each encompassing thousands of acres) and four pueblos were founded. The Indians were put to work supplying the menial labor for the new aristocracy. Most of them worked for Spanish Army veterans who had been granted the largest ranchos. The size of four of these cattle spreads was awesome. The San Pedro Rancho covered what are now the communities of Redondo Beach, Torrance, Wilmington, and Compton. Another covered all of Glendale and portions of Burbank, while a third and fourth made up huge chunks of Long Beach, Whittier, Anaheim, and also Santa Ana, Orange, Tustin, Costa Mesa, and a large section of Newport Beach.

This pastoral age for a privileged few was not to last; fed by fires of deep hostility to Spanish rule, Mexico launched a full-scale revolution, forcing Spain to grant her independence in 1822. California was now a province of Mexico. Unlike Spain, which had sought to keep foreign nations out of California while they exploited the new land, Mexico desired foreign trade. Cattle hides soon became the ''leather dollars'' of the Californians. The value of rancho lands increased in turn, as the demand for hides soared. The great land holdings of the missions were being eyed with covetous scrutiny. For those who looked toward the redistribution of the mission lands for their own financial gain, the Indians, who worked under the padres, became their wedge. A cry went up for the Indians' liberation and then for secularization of the missions. It would lead to a division of mission lands and a descent into poverty for the jobless Indians.

While the Mexicans were savoring the financial rewards of unrestricted trade and occupying themselves with internal intrigue, the American presence in California had been growing. Many Americans had traveled overland in the first stirrings of the westward movement, drawn by tales of easy riches and fertile lands. As would be the case throughout the history of westward expansion, what the Americans were desirous of, they would get. Early offers by the United States government to purchase the northern portion of California had been refused by Mexico; the refusal had only served to whet the Americans' appetite. Now they were prepared to take all of the state, in what they claimed was their manifest destiny.

President James Polk, fearing the French or British might also have designs on California, wasted no time in sending Captain John C. Fremont to conciliate the Californians, while secretly trying to foment a revolution in the province. By the time Mexican Governor Pio Pico voiced his uneasiness over American intentions, the threat had become a reality. In April of 1846 while Fremont was taking it upon himself to stir the northern California Yankees into a fighting frenzy, the Americans went to war with Mexico over the southern boundary of Texas.

The Mexicans were no match for the land-hungry Americans. Caught in a vice by the forces of Fremont descending from the north, Commodore Robert Stockton advancing inland from San Pedro, and General Stephen Kearny moving overland from New Mexico, the Mexicans surrendered California in January, 1847.

The dust had barely settled from the short-lived conflict when gold was discovered at Sutter's Mill in the Sacramento Valley. Its lure brought fortune seekers to California by the thousands. Beef, once raised for its hide, was now in demand as meat to feed a growing population. At 50 and 75 dollars a head, the hide trade gave way to the beef industry. The new wealth of the Angelenos was followed by an influx of unsavory characters looking to share in the boomtown riches. "Through the '50s and '60s," writes historian Remi Nadeau, "the city's wickedest reputation was unequaled on the coast, even including the California mines. . . . Pistol shots punctuated the atmosphere almost every night. Horse stealing, highway robbery, and murder became so commonplace that a temporary lull in the violence was a matter of news."

Eventually, many of the rancheros were put out of business, due to a loss of revenue because of saturation of the cattle market by herds driven into California from Missouri, Texas, and Mexico. To compound matters, a long period of drought forced the slaughtering of the few remaining animals for their hides. Now desperate, the once-prosperous Spanish families signed high interest mortgage loans on their land holdings. "Beset by American law, American taxes, (and) American usury," most of the aristocracy lost all they had accumulated to creditors and foreclosure. "The gringo," explains Nadeau, "had completed his conquest not by the barbarity of the sword, but with the civility of the sheriff's hammer."

With the breaking up of the ranchos' vast acreage, the sub-dividing turned ranchland into farmland. Attracted by the availability of 50-acre tracts for as little as ten dollars an acre on the installment plan, Northern Californians swarmed southward. Soon there was a mushrooming of towns—Santa Ana, Orange, Downey, Artesia, Tustin, Westminster, Santa Monica, Compton, San Fernando, Lompoc, Bakersfield, Tulare, Porterville, and Independence among them.

Los Angeles was undergoing a transformation as ancient adobes gave way to frame and brick structures. Pico House became the first building to reach three stories in the mid-1870s. South of First Street, gingerbread homes nestled among brightly colored gardens. Speeding the influx of emigrants to the city was the newly completed Southern Pacific railroad line from San Francisco, and not long after, the Santa Fe line from the East. A rate war saw railroad fares drop from a one-time high of more than $100 for those traveling from the Mississippi Valley to Los Angeles, to one dollar. People who had never entertained the notion of traveling suddenly found the idea of relocating appealing. The land boom of the '80s was underway.

The boom did not contain itself to Los Angeles alone; most of the southern coast from San Diego to Santa Barbara was affected. Whole towns seemed to spring up almost overnight, adding Burbank, Fullerton, Monrovia, Whittier, Inglewood, and Hollywood to the roster of rapidly spreading communities. Los Angeles was being advertised as a land of fertility. One real estate salesman put it: "You need not till the soil. You can look on while the earth sends forth her plenty.'' Other agents would describe any new townsite in glowing terms, no matter what the lay of the land. ''If the townsite was located on the desert,'' says Nadeau, ''it was billed as a health resort. If in a swamp, a magnificent new harbor was planned. On the side of a mountain, the view was superb.''

Despite a brief collapse in the land rush brought on by a tightening of speculative capital by the banks, Los Angeles' population continued to grow—from 11,000 in 1880, to 103,000 in 1897. By 1905, the Los Angeles basin contained more than 200,000 residents, due, in part, to the opening of the third railroad route from the east, the Union Pacific. The need for more water sent Angelenos searching for an additional source to supplement that of the Los Angeles River. It was found at the Owens River, flowing on the eastern side of the Sierra Nevada Mountains. A 250-mile gravity canal was laid to channel the water to the Los Angeles basin. Later, growth required tapping the Colorado River in 1941, and later still, the Feather River in Northern California.

Now, with a dependable source of water, Angelenos turned citrus growing into a multi-million dollar industry. In the early 1920s, oil was discovered at Signal Hill, the richness of its flow temporarily eclipsing even the lucrative Texas and Oklahoma fields. Hollywood was becoming the movie capital of the world, a glamour empire controlled by a handful of studios—20th Century-Fox, MGM, Warner Brothers, RKO, and Universal. By the mid-'30s, the aircraft industry had grown from a pile of nuts and bolts, scattered about the floor of an abandoned church in Santa Ana, to names destined to become household words during the war years—Lockheed, Douglas, North American Aviation, and Northrup among them.

From the 1940s to the '70s, Los Angeles' population figures jumped from a million-and-a-half to over three million. While the automobile became an all-consuming passion, the building of freeways allowed for a greater separation of home and work. Urban density increased as more Angelenos looked to escape the city's sprawl, a phenomenon in evidence today.

The New Downtown

Many Los Angeles residents still remember the old rooming houses that once lined Grand Avenue, near the heart of the city. They were two-story affairs, with massive banisters leading to a spacious porch. Originally built near the turn of the century, many of these houses first held the families of wealthy Easterners. Later, they became lodging for three, and sometimes four families, their once brightly painted exteriors allowed to weather to a drab gray. Until the late 1940s and early '50s, most of the residences surrounding the city's downtown area were of the same type—they would not survive for long. Increasing land values soon caused them to be bulldozed to rubble, remnants of a grand era turning to dust.

Though downtown Los Angeles was within walking distance from many of these dwellings, most families chose to ride the electric cars; giant, creaking conveyances of steel wheels and wooden seats. Powered by an overhead web of electric lines, these trolleys sported dual controls, allowing the conductor to change direction without turning the contraption around.

Los Angeles' downtown of the '40s was streets lined with rows of buildings, many with ornate stonework facades. Few of these structures rose more than ten or twelve stories, due to the 150-foot height restriction imposed because of earthquake fears. Huge awnings, overhanging the sidewalks, protected the passerby from the midday sun, or the occasional rainy day. The street intersections were controlled by clanging traffic signals, sporting extendable paddle-like signs painted with the words GO and STOP. Movie marquees advertised the latest Hollywood offering against a backdrop of flashing neon lights.

Sometimes, before shopping, a family would stop for lunch at Clifton's Cafeteria, its cool interior decorated with bubbling, rock-lined waterfalls. From the cafeteria's inside balcony, one could see the huge sign of the May Company department store. After lunch, the family might have headed for the Grand Central Public Market, between 3rd and 4th streets on Broadway. Here, amongst the fruit and vegetable-laden stalls, and the exotic aromas of rare spices, they could search for bargains. The voices of the produce hawkers could be heard above the din of the crowd. ''Hey, fresh corn, fresh corn. Hey, you want fresh tomatoes? I got fresh tomatoes.'' Taking his knife, a hawker would slice into the redness of a plump specimen, extending it for the prospective buyer to admire.

Back on the street, and loaded down with large shopping bags full of fresh produce, shoppers could see the white tower of the 32-story City Hall—the only building in downtown Los Angeles to exceed the 150-foot height restriction, and at the time, the tallest building in Southern California. Nearby, the Angels' Flight Railway could be seen traveling a short, steep grade to the top of Bunker Hill. Few Angelenos could know that, even then, the hill was being evaluated as the possible future site for a massive redevelopment project—a project so large, it would dwarf the older Los Angeles skyline.

Before the late 1950s, Los Angeles' growth had always been in the horizontal direction. But in 1957, the city's 150-foot height restriction was removed, and suddenly, the spreading metropolis began to show its shoulders. Along Wilshire Boulevard's Miracle Mile, the first of the city's skyscrapers began taking shape, the 22-story Lee Tower. As other new buildings continued to sprout along the boulevard, ''high-rises'' began appearing on Sunset Boulevard, and later, along Spring Street in the city's financial center. By the '60s, the financial district was spreading south and west in an explosion of new building projects. Near the Ambassador Hotel area of Beverly Hills and Westwood, the profusion of insurance and banking buildings soon seemed a separate city unto itself, all squeezed along a narrow 15½-mile corridor. Where once a foot of frontage land found along this stretch could be purchased for $100, it had risen to a price of $6,000.

In 1966, the first structure to rise as part of the Bunker Hill Urban Renewal Project was the 42-story Union Bank Building. In the same year, another 42-story tower, the Crocker Bank Building, designed by

William L. Pereira & Associates, rose above Sixth Street and Grand Avenue. The Bunker Hill area soon became a bedlam of activity. Giant cranes roared their diesel voices above the din of freeway traffic. Tons of excavated dirt filled endless caravans of trucks, as huge, block-size holes in the ground marked the locations of future monoliths. Like the upthrust of volcanically driven rock, rising to form an island above the ocean, the towers of Bunker Hill rose in quick succession from the previously bare landscape.

Today, downtown Los Angeles has gained much of its new look as a result of the Bunker Hill Redevelopment Project, attaining a prestige equal to an earlier time when the hill was covered with stately homes. Here, now, are the twin 52-story black towers shared by the Atlantic Richfield Company and the Bank of America. Beneath these tinted-glass giants, a subterranean shopping center provides Angelenos with endless hours of browsing pleasure, and a chance to savor the dining delights of its unique restaurants.

Another of the eye-catching structures on the Hill is the round, glass towers of the Bonaventure Hotel. A dazzling, mirror-like cluster of tubes, housing 1,500 rooms, glows fire-like as it reflects a sunset of melting golds and reds. Although it is not as flashy as the Bonaventure, the United California Bank's 62-story tower (Los Angeles' tallest) is still the most easily identifiable edifice on the downtown landscape.

Near ground level, there is the Los Angeles Music Center for the Performing Arts. Opened in 1965, the Center plays host to the annual Academy Awards and is famous for its theatrical and musical offerings. Actually a complex of three theatres, which includes the Dorothy Chandler Pavilion, the Mark Taper Forum, and the Ahmanson Theatre, the Center provides Angelenos with year-round entertainment. In the evening, the lights playing on the Forum highlight its rounded, bas-relief surface, making it a favorite subject for both amateur and professional photographers.

Amid downtown's beautifully landscaped malls, fountains, towering offices, apartments and hotels that have redefined Los Angeles' skyline, there is still the ambience of the older city. Due in part to the early preservation efforts of Mrs. Christine Sterling (a tireless champion of the city's heritage), El Pueblo de Los Angeles (the birthplace of Los Angeles) retains much the same look as when the buildings bordering its plaza were first raised. The oldest of the Pueblo's streets, Olvera, was recreated as a Mexican marketplace and opened in 1930. Here the aroma of spicy foods drifts through the displays of the street's colorful stalls, while buyers bargain for the best price on a piece of handmade pottery or a uniquely designed serape. A favorite item of children, the ''jumping bean,'' can be seen eliciting giggles as the small worm within moves in response to the heat of a child's cupped hand.

Elsewhere, the historic buildings of the Old Plaza area—the Pico House, the Merced Theatre, Sepulveda House, the Plaza Church, and others—serve as a backdrop for open-air concerts and colorful fiestas. The Plaza Church, erected three years after the founding of the city, then measured a diminutive 18 by 24 feet. It was later rebuilt in 1822, with more spacious proportions, and underwent further restoration after heavy rains in 1860 nearly destroyed its walls.

Another area of old town is Little Tokyo, a section bounded by Central Avenue, Los Angeles, and First and Second streets. Part of the largest Japanese community in the United States, Little Tokyo is a potpourri of small tea houses, restaurants, and tourist shops, offering imported ceramics to tailor-made kimonos. Just north of the Civic Center, along Broadway, New Chinatown covers a two-block area lined with small establishments selling Oriental wares, along with a number of restaurants and specialty food markets. Forced from its earlier site nearer to the city's center by plans for building a railroad terminal (Union Station) at the spot, Chinatown was reopened in 1939.

With a Los Angeles County population of more than two million Mexican-Americans, it is easy to understand why much of the language spoken in the central city area is Spanish. It has been said that Broadway is probably the largest ethnic shopping center in the country today. Here, on weekends, the Grand Central Market is a hive of agitated gesturing and rapid vocal exchanges conducted between Mexican, Guatemalan, and Colombian shoppers. Out on the street, while serenading shoppers with Spanish music drifting from their shops, vendors entice bargain hunters with colorful clothing displays.

The future face of Los Angeles' downtown only began to appear with the transformation of its Bunker Hill area; it is a process that is still continuing with at least a dozen new structures in various stages of completion, and others on the drawing board. When some of these projects are finished, nearly four million square feet of office space will lie within the vicinity of the Twin Towers.

One of the more ambitious projects will be the construction of the trapezoidal, 44- and 54-story towers of Crocker Center, destined for the Bunker Hill area in the early '80s. The development will occupy four acres and contain nearly 3½ million square feet of office, retail, and restaurant space. Another dramatic undertaking will be the Trust House Forte Hotel, planned for a 3¾ acre site between 3rd and 4th streets, along Figueroa. The windows in the face of this building will have the appearance of a great mirror, tilted so as to reflect the structure's neatly landscaped grounds and 12-story atrium. Included in the design will be tennis courts, a swimming pool, a health club, four movie theatres, and a number of shops and restaurants.

Due for completion in the autumn of 1981 is the 48-story Wells Fargo Building, planned for 5th and Flower streets. The structure will have estimated rental space of 890,000 square feet, and have its own helicopter landing pad. Other buildings now under construction, or ready to be occupied, are the first 140 units of The Promenade condominiums at 1st and Hope streets, and the Angelus Plaza, designed for senior citizens. Federally subsidized, the Plaza will be the second-largest development of its kind in the nation, containing 761 one-bedroom apartments.

Altogether, urban renewal projects in the Bunker Hill area will see some 800 mid-rise and high-rise condominiums sprout from the landscape. Combined with the added retail and office facilities now being planned, and a proposed Museum of Modern Art, Los Angeles' downtown may well become the model for other cities as it enters the 21st century.

Hollywood

"Hollywood is wonderful. Anyone who doesn't like it is either crazy or sober," said the mystery writer, Raymond Chandler. Chandler was only partly right, because "craziness" is what put Hollywood on the map. It took a kind of a crazy nerve to film 140 one-reelers a year, while using the town for a backdrop and its citizens as unsuspecting extras. Lured from New York and Chicago in the early 1900s by Los Angeles' abundant sunshine, the movie-makers would soon create the idols of the silver screen—those whose every action a world of impressionable young people would attempt to emulate.

One of the most brazen of these moviemakers, and a pioneer in the business, was Mack Sennett. An oft-told story of this genius will give one an idea as to what lengths moviemakers of the time were willing to go to film believable action footage. Sennett had hardly unpacked his equipment after arriving in Los Angeles to take over a studio near Glendale when he spotted a group of parading Shriners. Not having any particular movie plot in mind, but deciding the opportunity to use this crowd scene was too good to pass up, Sennett sent one of his crew to buy a large doll from a nearby department store. Grabbing his partner, Mabel Normand, Sennett gave her the doll and told her to run into the group of marchers while pleading for the father to show himself. While this was going on, Sennett's cameraman was catching it all on film. Finally, the poor girl's plea fell on sympathetic ears, and a Shriner left his place in line to offer his help. Suddenly, Ford Sterling, another of Sennett's group, rushed toward the poor Shriner and started an animated argument with him. By now the police had taken an interest in the armflailing scene. As they approached, Ford began yelling at them, then ran off. It was too much for these helmeted, brass-buttoned upholders of justice, and the chase was on. The scene was later to be incorporated into Sennett's first Keystone comedy.

The public was soon hungering for more than one-reelers, and on February 8, 1915, film director David Wark Griffith fed them his three-hour spectacle, *The Birth of a Nation*. The film had taken more than a year to produce, used thousands of extras, made use of innovative camera techniques, and swallowed every cent Griffith could squeeze out of his supporters. This film marked the "real birth" of the movies, and Hollywood soon became a household word.

By the mid-'40s, Hollywood was producing the majority of pictures made in America, as well as those throughout the rest of the world. Thousands of mothers were dragging curly-haired, dimple-cheeked babes to the city in hopes of launching them on a career to stardom. Older aspirants came without their mothers, in the hope of being discovered. Few succeeded, but Hollywood gained a collection of beautiful salesgirls and an array of suave parking-lot attendants.

It seemed inconceivable that the small black-and-white images, being produced on the screen of an in-home electric box, could threaten an industry that monopolized motion-picture theatres and the studios that ran them. Television came into the marketplace at a time when audiences were growing weary of films that seldom broached social issues. Television's impact nearly destroyed the Hollywood movie empire during the mid-'50s.

However, film producers remained strong. They decided to join in the new medium's success, converting their sound stages into television studios. Here they found a new empire to supplement the moneys of the old "dream factory." Today, the movie industry is still alive, but the concentration has been on "blockbusters" to bring in eight and nine figure money gates. Investments in some of these spectacles can run from 10 to 20 million dollars, but the returns can be fabulous, as when the movie *Jaws* reaped a nearly $119 million gross.

The largest of these motion picture-television mixes is Universal Studios. Its 420-acre back lot, with Old West, Mexican village, and New York tenement facades, can accommodate a number of film crews simultaneously. Unlike the old days when only the favored few could tour the inner sanctum of a Hollywood set, now more than four million guests are guided behind the scenes annually, where they witness a makeup artist at work, or are privy to some of the secrets of the special effects department. A two-hour tram ride will take you past an uncomfortably real-looking replica of a Great White shark (''Jaws''), which will try to devour a whole carload of sightseers. After this encounter with two tons of terrible teeth, the tour will continue with a visit to the ''Parting of the Red Sea'' and many other eye-openers.

Another interesting behind-the-scenes tour is the one offered by NBC (National Broadcasting System), at its studios in Burbank. Small groups are given a first-hand look at television shows in the making. Included in the tour are visits to the prop and wardrobe departments, and occasionally an encounter with a well-known personality.

When not occupied with the movie-making end of Hollywood, a visitor will enjoy viewing the life-size wax figures of movie personalities, displayed at the Hollywood Wax Museum on Hollywood Boulevard. Or they might prefer visiting the area's bookstores, specializing in new or used books, offering hours of browsing pleasure. Then too, there is Mann's Chinese Theatre with its ornate, temple-like facade, and nearly six decades of movieland celebrities' hand and foot-prints decorating its entrance. While on West Third Street and Fairfax Avenue, the Farmers Market makes food shopping a pleasure, with its artistically arranged fruits and vegetables, imported and domestic gourmet items, unique gift shops, and the international delicacies of its many fine restaurants.

A visitor will soon discover that Hollywood is really more than what is within the 14.5-square-mile-area on the charts of the City Planning Commission. ''Geographically,'' writes W.W. Robinson in *Los Angeles: A Profile*, ''Hollywood's boundaries are today completely elastic. . . . (It has come) to mean any place in Southern California where motion picture people (live) and (work), whether in Los Angeles, Culver City, Beverly Hills, Santa Monica, Malibu, or the San Fernando Valley.''

Although some of Hollywood's actors still live within the district's limits, most have chosen to divorce themselves from the accumulation of tinsel and adoring fans, to seek a more reclusive lifestyle behind the manicured hedges of Beverly Hills, Bel Air, or Brentwood. Beverly Hills, more than any other area of movieland, exudes the strongest mystique to those seeking to catch a glimpse of the wealthy. Here, property values can run into the millions.

''Insofar as it can be weighed, measured, observed, and interpreted,'' says the writer Walter Wagner in his book *Beverly Hills: Inside the Golden Ghetto*, ''society in Beverly Hills numbers four loosely knit, fluctuating and overlapping categories—the idle rich, the do-gooder rich, the getting-on-in years-movie-star rich, and the nouveaux rich.''

The key word here is *rich*, an adjective that tends to blur any distinctions in the above catagories. And where there is an abundance of such riches, so too, are there usually places nearby that stock the things the rich desire. Beverly Hills' Rodeo Drive falls in this category, as do the neighboring areas of Century City, Westwood, Culver City, and Marina del Rey. Necessities for the rich run from Ethiopian jewelry to distinctive signature labels attached to the finest in men's and women's apparel, a life-size brass chimpanzee, a bronze garden faucet, lapis lazuli in rings, diamonds, and other precious gems woven through heavy gold chains, and the smatterings of color to brighten up a certain hallway, such as a small Picasso, Dali, or Chagall.

Hollywood still has its original glitter, it has just been spread a little thinner.

Old Town Plaza

Exposition Park, U.S.C. campus

Marineland, in Palos Verdes
(Previous page) The city at evening from Mt. Wilson

The Ambassador Hotel

The Anaheim Stadium

The lighthouse on Palos Verdes peninsula

Los Angeles International Airport

Occidental College

Hollywood Hills

Downtown, from Pershing Square

CITY NATIONAL BANK
ONE WILSHIRE
ONE WILSHIRE

The Hollywood Bowl

Parker Center

Marina del Rey

San Gabriel Mountains

The Queen Mary, Long Beach

The Dorothy Chandler Pavilion at the Music Center

Fisherman's Village at Marina del Rey

University of California, Irvine Campus

Federal Building

The Japanese Garden in Descanso Gardens, La Canada
(Following pages) Lupins in bloom, Angeles National Forest

Long Beach

Hollywood Park Race Track

Laguna Beach

Newport Beach

Laguna Beach

Griffith Observatory

FRESH ROASTED PEANUTS
FRESH SEASONED POPCORN
KNOTTS
ring 20s Airfield

Newport Beach

Knott's Berry Farm, Buena Park

Huntington Gardens, San Marino

Downtown, from the Convention Center

Los Angeles Memorial Coliseum

Palisade Park, Santa Monica, at sunset
(Preceding pages) Los Angeles from the Griffith Park Observatory

致青
NEW CHINA TOWN
GOLDEN PALACE
RESTAURANT
911 N. BROADWAY
ONE BLOCK
LUNCH - DINNER
BANQUETS
DON'T
WALK
CHINESE DISHES
OPEN

Entrance to Olvera Street

Entrance to Chinatown

Ambassador Auditorium, Pasadena

The promenade, Palisade Park, Santa Monica

Coastline at Palos Verdes

Beverly Hills City Hall

Corona del Mar coastline

Union Station

Mark Taper Forum

City Hall, Pasadena

Eastern Canal, Venice

Mt. Baldy, Angeles National Forest

Echo Park

Los Angeles City Hall

The Harbor Freeway and downtown Los Angeles skyline at sunset
(Following pages) Laguna Beach

Palos Verdes looking toward Redondo Beach

Disneyland

CBS Television

74

CBS
TELEVISION CITY

Von Kleinschmid Center, U.S.C. campus

Ports O ' Call Village, San Pedro

The GALLEON
MEDITERRANEAN
IMPORTS
ANTHONY
KANE'S
SUPER SHIRTS
HALLMARK
HOUSE
Gifts
TOY SHOPPE

PERSEUS

A view of downtown Long Beach, from the Convention Center

Fisherman's Village, Marina del Rey

The Biltmore Hotel, from Pershing Square

The Bradbury Building, downtown Los Angeles

MacArthur Park

The San Fernando Mission

Pepperdine University at Malibu
(Preceding pages) The city lights of Los Angeles at sunset
from the planetarium

Farmers Market

FARMERS
MARKET
FARMERS
MARKET
Walter Wright
CONTEMPORARY JEWELRY
SPEED
LIMIT
5

Modern Los Angeles architecture and the Bank of America Towers

Palm Springs resort

FIGUEROA ST.
2500 S

The Rose Bowl, Pasadena

St. Vincent Church

The Lummis House

Laguna Beach

Los Angeles Planetarium

Desert scene outside of Los Angeles

CNA Building

San Pedro, a view of the fishing fleet

LOS ANGELES ZOO

The San Fernando Valley

The entrance to the Los Angeles Zoo

Mission San Gabriel

Ocotillo cactus in the desert outside of Los Angeles

The Forum at Inglewood
(Following pages) Sunrise at Joshua Tree National Monument

The Bonaventure Hotel

J. Paul Getty Art Museum, Malibu
(Preceding page) The Japanese Garden in Huntington Botanical Gardens, San Marino
(Second preceding page) View of the city from Mulholland Drive

Santa Barbara Mission

The Los Angeles Historical and Art Museum
(Following page) Sunset at Aliso Beach

The twin towers of Century City

The U.C.L.A. Library from Royce Hall
(Preceding page) Beverly Hills

The Music Center Fountain and City Hall

Sunset Strip, Hollywood
(Preceding pages) Los Angeles from the Baldwin Hills

Japanese Village Plaza

MITSUBISHI BANK
Japanese Village Plaza
日本村広場

The Brown Derby Restaurant on Wilshire Boulevard

Los Angeles Arboretum

Flag Mall and the Los Angeles City Hall

Whittier College

Hollywood

A Beverly Hills park, across from the Beverly Hills Hotel

The Santa Anita Race Track

The ''Miracle Mile'' on Wilshire Boulevard

PRUDENTIAL
CALIFORNIA FEDERAL
KFAC
Dennison

FORD'S HARDWARE
Universal Studios Glamor Tram
Universal Studios Glamor Tram
Universal Studios Glamor Tram

Culture on
the Grand Scale

Many an Angeleno was first introduced to the cultural scene of Los Angeles when just a child. It generally happened while on a field trip with a grammar school class. After studying about the bones of great prehistoric beasts uncovered from Los Angeles' La Brea Tar Pits, the class would go to the Los Angeles County Museum of History, Science and Art at Exposition Park to see the bones first hand. Within the coolness of the museum's enormous hushed halls, the class would be led past marble statuary, through a darkened room of exquisitely detailed animal displays, and then would emerge into a brightly lit wing of the museum to find the room dominated by the massive skeletal reconstruction of an imperial mammoth.

The children might not have known it at the time, but they were looking at one of the world's largest Pleistocene skeletal collections. Here, the carefully assembled remains of a specimen collection, containing nearly half a million bones, delighted and amazed onlookers. Since 1913, when the museum's scientists first began recovering these bones from the tar pits located along Wilshire Boulevard, they had pieced together part of the fauna history of ancient Los Angeles. Besides the mammoths' bones, which had been preserved by the tar, the children could view those of saber-toothed cats, of flying creatures with 12-foot wing spans, and countless other specimens. For days after this visit, many might be found checking the locks on bedroom windows before burying their heads under the covers—the image of gruesome tiger fangs a fresh memory. Since that time, the museum has broken into separate institutions. The science portion is now housed nearby in the California Museum of Science and Industry, while the art collection has found a home in the multi-building complex that makes up the Los Angeles County Museum of Art, located in Hancock Park next to the La Brea Tar Pits. Opened in 1965, the new art museum was built with 12 million dollars in funds raised by private citizens.

Another huge repository of art is located on the estate of the one-time Pacific Electric Railway tycoon, Henry E. Huntington. During the early 1900s, Huntington had almost single-handedly put Los Angeles on wheels. At the time, his vast network of electric cars covered more area and generated more dollars per mile than any other electric interurban system in the world. Huntington's wealth allowed him to accumulate some of the world's finest literary and art treasures, housing them in two massive marble buildings on 200 beautifully landscaped acres in San Marino. Preferring to have his magnificent collection of more than half a million books and five million manuscripts available to scholars, and to have British art works of the 18th and 19th centuries available for all the public to enjoy, Huntington willed his estate to the people. Here, close behind the massive wrought-iron gates that mark the estate's entrance on Oxford Road, stands the Library Building. Within its dimly lit halls (a precaution against light's tendency to fade colors) one can view changing exhibitions of some of the rarest of rare books. Included in the displays are a 1410 rendering of Chaucer's *Canterbury Tales*, Franklin's *Autobiography*, Thoreau's *Walden*, Poe's *Annabel Lee*, and the book that marked the beginnings of printing with moveable type—the *Gutenberg Bible* on vellum.

In the nearby Art Gallery (originally the Huntington residence), French 18th-century decorative art mingles with British paintings, drawings, sculpture and furniture of the same period. The highlight of this display is Thomas Gainsborough's ''Blue Boy'' and Sir Thomas Lawrence's ''Pinkie.'' Bathed in subdued overhead lighting, the world-famous couple stare at one another from their ornate, gold frames.

Of the many gardens that add color to the Huntington grounds, two, the Desert Garden and the Japanese Garden, are perhaps the most memorable. The Desert Garden covers twelve acres on the estate's southeast corner and contains the largest outdoor collection of desert plants in the world. Among the more than 25,000 plants is a 1,000-pound golden barrel cactus, and many pincushion cacti measuring more than three feet in diameter. The Japanese Garden, a ¼-mile walk

The La Brea Tar Pits

Los Angeles City Hall

west of the main entrance, is a blending of five acres of Japanese plants, stone ornaments, a furnished Japanese House, and a picturesque, red-colored moon bridge, spanning a small pond.

On West Colorado Boulevard, in nearby Pasadena, another self-made millionaire has created a monument to his assorted taste in art. What had formally been the Pasadena Art Museum is now the Norton Simon Museum of Art. In the short time since Simon has taken over the building, he has dramatically altered a collection that was originally devoted to contemporary art. Giving the collection a broader range, Simon has installed several hundred million dollars worth of Old Masters, highlights of which are Rembrandt's *Portrait of the Artist's Son*, *Titus*, Ruben's *David and Goliath*, Tiepolo's *Triumph of Virtue and Fortitude*, Goya's *Saint Jerome*, and a recent addition for which Simon's wife (actress Jennifer Jones) paid a reported $3.7 million—Dirk Bouts' 15th-century masterpiece, *Resurrection of Christ*.

In addition, Simon has acquired at least 200 pieces of sculpture from ancient India, Thailand, and Cambodia. The prize of this collection is a 44-inch bronze figure of the god Shiva, purchased from a New York dealer for a million dollars. Though not especially popular at this time with many of the museum's visitors, the Indian religious art nevertheless meets Simon's immutable standards, which he concedes, counts for more with him than popular taste.

The late billionaire, J. Paul Getty, was another art collector not swayed by popular taste. His love for early Greek, Roman, and Etruscan art led to the construction of the J. Paul Getty Museum in the coastal community of Malibu. In this replica of a Roman villa, Getty housed his favorite acquisitions, whether Etruscan, or fine examples of French 18th-century furniture and early 1900 Western European paintings.

Not all of the culture of Los Angeles is housed behind glass cases or hung on the walls of great museums; the city is also a showcase for the best in theatrical and musical entertainment. Los Angeles first gained prominence for its dramatic and concert fare during the 1870s-80s with performances given at the Merced Theatre, Turnverein Hall, the Grand Opera House, and Hazard's Pavilion. As the city entered the 20th century, its musical development was given impetus by the producer L.E. Behymer, bringing top musical entertainers of the day to play at the Burbank Theatre, the Los Angeles Theatre, and Hazard's Pavilion. It was with Behymer's help that the indefatigable Artie Mason Carter realized her dream of giving Los Angeles an outdoor theatre, the Hollywood Bowl, where Angelenos were treated to the first of the famous ''Symphonies Under the Stars.''

The most spectacular boost for the Los Angeles music and drama scene in recent years has been the completion (in 1967) of its Music Center for the Performing Arts. The first structure of this three-building complex, the Dorothy Chandler Pavilion, was finished in 1964 and named for the lady most responsible for its conception, and of raising the funds necessary for its completion. Designed to hold 1,500 people, the Pavilion has excellent acoustics, which allow every theatre-goer full enjoyment of its symphonic programs or musical comedies. The center's other two buildings, the Mark Taper Forum and the Ahmanson Theatre, are devoted to experimental drama and plays of wider audience appeal.

In addition to this glittering Music Center complex, Angelenos have the choice of attending countless other large and small theatres, many of which have attracted highly creative choreographers, instrumentalists, and actors, to a city growing in theatrical accomplishments. But all is not emigrant talent. Los Angeles is turning out its own talent, with musical and operatic workshops given at U.C.L.A. and other colleges city-wide.

Book lovers will find the city's rare book market second only to that of New York. Spread throughout the Hollywood district, and in posh establishments dotting the Beverly Hills and Westwood areas, specialty bookshops supply a knowledgeable and growing trade. Some of these bookstores cover a wide spectrum of collecting interests, supplying both new and long out-of-print material to a scholarly clientele. Others of these shops specialize in only one or two fields of collector interest, such as science fiction and fantasy, or nautical lore. A number of these establishments are open to buyers only by appointment, their small, beautifully bound and illustrated collections being too valuable for casual handling.

Every other year, the California Book Fair is held in Los Angeles, drawing members of the Antiquarian Booksellers Association of America (ABAA) from many states, and other dealers from as far as England

and Canada. Here, displayed under one roof, are books ranging from the moderately priced collector's item, to extreme rarities. The combined specialized book knowledge of the nearly 80 dealers attending this "bibliomaniacs delight" would make the staff of many a learned institution blush.

Commercial art galleries are also part of the cultural scene. Along La Cieniga Boulevard, and in the Westwood and Brentwood areas, mini-museums are experiencing a renaissance of collector interest. Some of these galleries show and sponsor California artists exclusively; others feature works by Mexican Masters, or established 20th-century artists such as Calder, Miro, Marini, Chagall, and Paul Jenkins. Still others provide the discriminating buyer with beautiful works of stained glass, ceramics, weavings, and semi-precious stone carvings.

Combine all of the above pursuits with trips to the city's historically innovative structures, such as those designed by the master architect Frank Lloyd Wright, planetarium shows at the Griffith Park Observatory, and numerous outdoor markets displaying the wares of talented craftsmen, and the myth of Los Angeles as a cultural desert should forever be dispelled.

Los Angeles County Museum of Art

Signal Hill

A Sampling of Suburbs

Angelenos who owned cars during the '40s can remember the difficulties they faced when traveling from the city's central portions to its suburbs. To reach any of Los Angeles' outlying areas required traveling for what seemed like hours, through a maze of streets and past countless intersections. With more cars pouring into the Basin each day, it was inevitable that a way would be found to more quickly move the growing snarl of traffic, threading its way through the city's vast checkerboard of intersecting streets. A part of that solution had been in operation since December of 1940. It was the first freeway to be built in California (and in the United States), and connected downtown Los Angeles with the city of Pasadena.

Because of building restrictions during wartime, Angelenos had to wait a number of years before additional links could be added to the Arroyo Seco Parkway (now the Pasadena Freeway) in what had been envisioned as a freeway complex. But by the end of the '40s, work on the Harbor, Santa Ana, San Bernardino, and Hollywood freeways was in full swing. No longer would Angelenos have to fight the endless miles of stop-and-go traffic that overheated cars and tempers.

Eventually, the links began to join, and today Los Angeles is criss-crossed by over 30 freeways, totaling some 1,500 miles. Congestion is still a problem for the freeway traveler, especially when an accident has blocked a portion of these arterials during peak traffic hours. But most Angelenos have learned to take the delays in stride, knowing that freeways are safer and faster than the surface streets and allow for a quick escape to the mountains, seashore, forests, or desert. More importantly, the mobility provided by this great web of inter-connecting concrete pathways has allowed Angelenos their choice of living area. It is the freeways, more than any other factor, that have accelerated Los Angeles' massive urban growth.

This growth has divided itself, roughly, into five large regions—central, northeastern, northwestern, southern, and Orange County—as a combination, better known as Greater Los Angeles. As is the case in other large metropolitan areas, some of these regions also define sections of ethnic concentrations. Estimates state that more than a quarter of Los Angeles County's population is Hispanic, and that the majority of the city's public school enrollees have Spanish surnames.

To the south, past the communities of Torrance and Carson, lies the beautiful Palos Verdes Peninsula, known for its expensive homes and sweeping ocean view. Just to the east, the Port of Los Angeles and the Port of Long Beach form the world's largest manmade harbor. Within the harbor's nine-mile breakwater are more than 50 miles of developed waterfront—a maze of channels and inlets. In 1899, after a long, drawn-out battle between those who wanted a port to be built at Santa Monica, and those who favored a more southern location, the winners saw the first barge of rock dumped to begin the new harbor's breakwater at San Pedro. Since that day, the two ports have become leaders in the amount of tonnage handled annually, and a favorite with visitors seeking a unique shopping and dining experience at the area's Ports-of-Call and Whaler's Wharf.

At the northwestern end of the Greater Los Angeles coastline, the Santa Monica Mountains extend inland, nearly cutting the city in half from west to east. Here is an extraordinary platform for viewing almost all of this huge metropolis. At night, from along Mulholland Drive, running the length of the mountain's ridge, one can see the San Fernando Valley glittering with bright pockets of light. Far to the northeast, a fainter chain of lights traces Foothill Boulevard, at the base of the San Gabriel Mountains, where it passes through the communities of Sunland, Tujunga, La Crescenta, La Canada, and into the brighter glow that marks the city of Pasadena. To the east and southeast, boulevard lights cut straight paths through the Hollywood, Beverly Hills, and Westwood areas, then lose their identities as they melt into the city's center.

Here, snuggled in the canyons of the Santa Monica Mountains, beautiful mansions dot the landscape. However, life has not been all sunshine for these Olympian dwellers. The mountain and canyon areas have experienced their share of natural disasters. Over the last 20 years, thousands of acres of this paradise have been denuded by fires from the dryness and heat of summer. Winter has dealt an equally disastrous blow by dropping heavy rains, leaving the residents to deal with mud flows and slides. But one should not be discouraged. These instances are isolated and overshadowed by the usual year-around sunshine. This sunshine, the good economic opportunities, and lush parks and playgrounds for children are the area's strengths, as in other Los Angeles suburbs.

Dodger Stadium, Chavez Ravine

Fisherman's Village, Marina del Rey

Port d' Italy
WINES & ITALY
BEERS & ALES
ITALIAN
RESTAURANT
ORANGE JULIUS

Playgrounds
in Paradise

Since its opening in 1955, Disneyland has become a monument to one man's personal dream—that of building the world's greatest amusement park for the pleasure of children and adults alike. The man was Walt Disney, who John L. Chapman described in his book *Incredible Los Angeles* as, "... the biggest and most durable one-man show in modern Southern California enterprise, mayor of the Magic Kingdom, the prince of imagination, architect of childhood dreams and fairy tales, keeper of the animal world, defender of truth and purity, (and) maker of merry."

No matter what a first time visitor's preconceptions are of this sprawling fantasyland of fun (25 miles southeast of Los Angeles in the community of Anaheim), they will fall short of reality. For at Disneyland, the suspension of disbelief begins at its gates, without a visitor being aware of it. Day or night, one can board a jungle boat in "Adventureland" and take a watery safari through elephant, alligator, and gorilla territory. Or if a visitor prefers, the riverboat *Mark Twain* will ferry him through the haunts of Tom Sawyer and Davy Crockett, in "Frontierland."

Crossing the drawbridge of Sleeping Beauty's Castle, the world of "Fantasyland" awaits those perpetual youngsters who believe in Peter Pan or the always-tardy rabbit of Alice's Wonderland. Here is the mighty Matterhorn, a 14-story mountain containing a hair-raising bobsled ride. Though more reality than fantasy, "Tomorrowland" may appear so to those visitors transported through its exciting world of science. The submarine voyage will take them on a trip to the depths of our watery world, where afterwards, they can board a spaceship for the flight to the moon and then explore the mysteries of inner space. Nearby, the excitement of haunted mansions and pugnacious pirates await one's trip to New Orleans Square. While in the rollicking world of "Bear Country," you come face to face with characters like Liverlips McGrowl.

If Disneyland fails to drain all your energy, the wild west setting of Knott's Berry Farm in Buena Park is just ten minutes away. From its humble beginnings as a real berry farm, Walter Knott's boysenberry patch has grown into California's second-greatest amusement attraction. Here, 150 acres are filled with the authentically recreated structures of an old California mining town, the thrilling rides of a Roaring '20s amusement area, and the spicy aromas of south-of-the-border dishes wafting through the streets of the Farm's Fiesta Village. Old Mr. Knott may never have envisioned corkscrew roller coasters zooming through 360° loops, or 20-story parachute jumps towering above a motorcycle chase race course when he erected the first ghost town buildings around his Chicken Dinner Restaurant, but he aimed to amuse the public, and so he has.

Another of Buena Park's attractions is the Japanese Village. Modeled somewhat after a similar park in Nara, Japan, it is a peaceful setting of colorful pavilions where tame deer wander about the grounds taking handouts from the visitors. Underfoot, the cooing of white doves elicits displays of peacock vanity, as the tails of these huge birds spread to reveal their iridescent plumage. Here, also, black swans float serenely upon the waters of the park's lagoon, as visitors sip tea in a classic Teahouse.

Before leaving the Buena Park area, any dedicated movie-goer will find a visit to the Movieland Wax Museum a special treat. Over 200 movie stars of the past and present are immortalized here in disturbingly lifelike wax figures. Ever since 1962, when the famed actress Mary Pickford was chosen to host the opening ceremonies for Movieland, there has been a steady stream of visitors (over a million annually) from all parts of the United States and abroad, coming to view their favorite stars. The price of admission also allows one to tour the Palace of Living Art. Here, famous paintings are recreated in life-size wax figures. Mona Lisa, Blue Boy, and Whistler's Mother are among the many so produced, in addition to a marble copy of Michelangelo's "Pieta."

During July and August of each year, the Pageant of the Masters is staged at Laguna Beach's Festival of Arts. Here again, three-dimensional sets recreate famous paintings and sculpture, but these figures are not wax; they are citizens of the Laguna Beach community. As night settles over the 2,572-seat Irvine Bowl, its stage is suddenly lit with carefully arranged lights, and a 16th-century work-of-art glows with astonishing realism. In this case, it is the ornate, gold and enamel saltcellar of Francis I, crafted by the famed Italian metalworker, Benvenuto Cellini. Covered with gold body paint, two models hold rigid poses, while the stage lighting adds the finishing touches to this Vienna Museum masterpiece.

Once again the stage darkens, and when lit a few minutes later, the audience is treated to a festival favorite, da Vinci's *Last Supper*. The amphitheatre is hushed; it is as if the great fresco has sprung to life with the rich colors of its pre-deteriorated splendor. A backstage look would present another picture of this religious enactment. Instead of the beautifully draped garments one views from the audience position, mis-matched rags are seen covering the participants. Faces are streaked with different colors of body paint, creating artificial shadow areas. Lighting, dress, body paint; all have been put together to present a superb illusion.

As one travels up the coast from Laguna, fun-in-the-sun awaits the visitor at any of the beach stops along the way. Yacht clubs and unique shopping districts mark the Balboa-Newport Beach area, while farther ahead, surfers remind visitors that they are in the home of the summer international surfing competition at Huntington Beach. From Seal Beach to San Pedro, activity along the coastline increases. Visitors can spend an afternoon taking in the rides at the Long Beach Amusement Park, and later visit the ocean liner *Queen Mary*—a floating palace at the Port of Long Beach's Pier J.

Perched on the tip of the Palos Verdes peninsula, Hanna-Barbera's Marineland is a water circus of somersaulting dolphins, leaping "killer whales" and ball-playing seals. Its newly completed Baja Reef is unique among theme parks, offering a chance to actually immerse oneself in the environment of the fish population. Donning bathing suit, mask, snorkel, and fins (provided by the park for a small charge) a visitor can mingle with the schools of ocean fish, which inhabit this underwater paradise.

However, there are other tanks here where the residents are not so friendly. In "Passages Beneath the Sea," inhabitants of the deep can be seen through underwater windows, occasionally edging against the glass to get a better look at curious visitors.

Far to the northeast of these coastal communities, near the foothills of the San Gabriel Mountains, lies Arcadia's 127-acre Los Angeles State and County Arboretum. The ornate Queen Anne Cottage decorates the shore of the Arboretum's lagoon. Originally owned by a wealthy Californian, the century-old house is now an historical landmark. Plants from many areas of the world bloom here in profusion. Peacocks strut the grounds, their tail colorings providing additional beauty to the myriads of bright flowers displayed in the Arboretum's many gardens.

Closer to central Los Angeles, the Memorial Coliseum in Exposition Park can seat up to 95,000 ardent football fans of U.S.C. and U.C.L.A. home games. At other times, the stadium is filled with excited track and field buffs. Next door, a modern indoor Sports Arena sees capacity crowds gather to watch championship boxing matches, tennis tournaments, track meets, and professional basketball games.

For those visitors to the San Fernando Valley, a giant 200-acre entertainment complex, known as Magic Mountain, offers excitement of the thrills-and-spills kind. While the children are sent scampering through Children's World, to play amid its creative recreation complex, the adults can hit the big rides. Four roller coasters get the old adrenalin flowing, while the Log Jammer, splashing down a water-filled viaduct, will cool the brows of those who dared to take on all four.

If you still have the stomach for it, food is available everywhere. The aroma of country-fried chicken mixes with that of piping hot pizza, which in turn mingles with the smell of sizzling steaks. Elsewhere, a perpetual Oktoberfest offers Bavarian delicacies, and at La Cantina, there is the spicier fare of authentic Mexican food. Entertainment is plentiful too, with contemporary rock bands playing day-and-night concerts for an appreciative, younger audience. And for those who like to sit while the entertainment does the moving, the Toyota Showcase Theatre offers big name celebrities.

From skiing its snow-capped mountains, to plunging into the surf, Los Angeles is "Fun City, U.S.A."

(Following page) Griffith Park

Beautiful America Publishing Company

The nation's foremost publisher of quality color photography

Current Books

Alaska	Maryland	Oregon Vol. II
Arizona	Massachusetts	Oregon Coast
Boston	Michigan	Oregon Country
British Columbia	Michigan Vol. II	Pacific Coast
California	Minnesota	Pennsylvania
California Vol. II	Missouri	Pittsburgh
California Coast	Montana	San Diego
California Desert	Montana Vol. II	San Francisco
California Missions	Monterey Peninsula	San Juan Islands
California Mountains	Mormon	Seattle
Chicago	Mt. Hood (Oregon)	Tennessee
Colorado	Nevada	Texas
Dallas	New Jersey	Utah
Delaware	New Mexico	Utah Country
Denver	New York	Vancouver U.S.A.
Florida	New York City	Vermont
Georgia	Northern California	Virginia
Hawaii	Northern California Vol. II	Volcano Mt. St. Helens
Idaho	North Carolina	Washington
Illinois	North Idaho	Washington Vol. II
Indiana	Ohio	Washington, D.C.
Kentucky	Oklahoma	Wisconsin
Las Vegas	Orange County	Wyoming
Los Angeles, 200 Years	Oregon	Yosemite National Park

Forthcoming Books

Alabama	Kauai	Oahu
Arkansas	Maine	Phoenix
Baltimore	Maui	Rhode Island
Connecticut	Mississippi	Rocky Mountains
Detroit	New England	South Carolina
The Great Lakes	New Hampshire	South Dakota
Houston	North Dakota	West Virginia
Kansas		

Large Format, Hardbound Books

Beautiful America	Beauty of Washington	Lewis & Clark Country
Beauty of California	Glory of Nature's Form	Western Impressions
Beauty of Oregon	Volcanoes of the West	

(Preceding page) Loyola University